This collection of quotations is dedicated to all the great women whose words have motivated, inspired and brought tears and laughter into our lives.

This book was compiled by someone who truly believes in the power of words and how they can impact feelings and attitudes.
We hope you enjoy the quotations as much as we do.

"I gain strength, courage and confidence by every experience in which I must stop and look fear in the face...
I say to myself, I've lived through this and can take the next thing that comes along...
We must do the things we think we cannot do."

Eleanor Roosevelt

"I never notice
what has been done.
I only see what
remains to be done."

Madam Curie

"Far away there in the sunshine are my highest aspirations. I may not reach them, but I can look up and see their beauty, believe in them and try to follow where they lead."

Louisa May Alcott

"Every great mistake has a halfway moment, a split second when it can be recalled and perhaps remedied."

Pearl S. Buck

"Being powerful is like being a lady. If you have to tell people you are, you aren't."

Margaret Thatcher

"To love what you do and feel that it matters—how could anything be more fun?"

Katherine Graham

"The first problem for all of us, men and women, is not to learn, but to unlearn."

Gloria Steinem

"Don't be humble:
you're not
that great."

Golda Meir

"From birth to age 18,
a girl needs good parents,
from 18 to 35 she needs good
looks, from 35 to 55 she
needs a good personality, and
from 55 on she needs cash."

Sophie Tucker

"Yesterday is
a cancelled check;
tomorrow is
a promissory note;
today is
the only cash you have—
so spend it wisely."

Kay Lyons

"Men, their rights and nothing more; women, their rights and nothing less."

Susan B. Anthony

"... perhaps one has
to be very old before
one learns how to be
amused rather than
shocked."

Pearl S. Buck

"Nothing in life
is to be feared.
It is only
to be understood."

Madame Curie

"Opportunities are usually disguised by hard work, so most people don't recognize them."

Ann Landers

"It is not fair to ask of others what you are not willing to do yourself."

Eleanor Roosevelt

"Courage is the price
that life exacts for
granting peace."

Amelia Earhart

"After the verb
'To Love', 'To Help'
is the most beautiful
verb in the world."

Bertha von Suttner

"We've chosen the path to equality, don't let them turn us around."

Geraldine A. Ferraro

"We are not interested in the possibilities of defeat."

Queen Victoria

W19

"I am only one;
But still I am one.
I cannot do everything,
but still I can do
something; I will not
refuse to do the
something I can do."

Helen Keller

"Loneliness is the most terrible poverty"

Mother Teresa

"You have to accept whatever comes and the only important thing is that you meet it with courage and with the best you have to give."

Eleanor Roosevelt

"We fought hard.
 We gave it our best.
 We did what was right.
 And we made a difference."

Geraldine A Ferraro

"Aerodynamically the
bumble bee shouldn't
be able to fly, but the
bumble bee doesn't know it
so it goes on flying
anyway."

Mary Kay Ash

"The more I traveled the more I realized that fear makes strangers of people who should be friends."

Shirely MacLain

"God knows
(She knows) that
women try."

Gloria Steinem

"In passing, also, I would like to say that the first time Adam had a chance he laid the blame on women."

Lady Nancy Astor

"Success can make you go
one of two ways.
It can make you a
prima donna, or it
can smooth the edges,
take away the insecurities,
let the nice things
come out."

Barbara Walters

"I've never sought success in order to get fame and money; it's the talent and the passion that count in success."

Ingrid Bergman

"A happy woman is one who has no cares at all; a cheerful woman is one who has cares but doesn't let them get her down."

Beverly Sills

"We all live with the objective of being happy; our lives are all different and yet the same."

Anne Frank

"The most exciting thing about women's liberation is that this century will be able to take advantage of talent and potential genius that have been wasted because of taboos."

Helen Reddy

"It is worse than folly...
not to recognize the truth,
for in it lies the tinder
for tomorrow."

Pearl S. Buck

"When you cease to make a contribution you begin to die."

Eleanor Roosevelt

"Those who do not know how to weep with their whole heart don't know how to laugh either."

Golda Meir

"Self-expression must pass into communication for its fulfillment."

Pearl S. Buck

"God does not ask your ability or your inability. He asks only your availability."

Mary Kay Ash

"Don't compromise yourself.
You are all you've got."

Betty Ford

"Character contributes to beauty. It fortifies a woman as her youth fades.
A mode of conduct, a standard of courage, discipline, fortitude and integrity can do a great deal to make a woman beautiful.

Jaqueline Bisset

"Men have always detested women's gossip because they suspect the truth: their measurments are being taken and compared."

Erica Jong

"I've had an exciting life;
I married for love and
got a little money
along with it."

Rose Kennedy

"This became a credo of mine...attempt the impossible in order to improve your work."

Bette Davis

"Let the world know you as
you are, not as you think
you should be, because
sooner or later, if you
are posing, you will
forget the pose, and
then where are you?"

Fanny Brice

"The future belongs
to those who believe
in the beauty of
their dreams."

Eleanor Roosevelt

"...you don't get to choose how you're going to die, or when. You can only decide how you're going to live. Now!"

Joan Baez

"You grow up the day you have your first real laugh— at yourself."

Edith Barrymore

"When people say:
She's got everything.
I've only one answer:
I haven't had
tomorrow."

Elizabeth Taylor

"...love is the only thing that we can carry with us when we go, and it makes the end so easy."

Louisa May Alcott

"Trouble is a part of life,
and if you don't share it,
you don't give the person
who loves you a chance to
love you enough."

Dinah Shore

"People who fight fire with fire usually end up with ashes."

Abigail VanBuren

"You cannot shake hands with a clenched fist."

Indira Gandhi

"Whether women are
better than men
I cannot say—
but I can say
they are certainly
no worse."

Golda Meir

"It isn't the common man at all who is important; it's the uncommon man."

Lady Nancy Astor

"In spite of the cost
of living, it's
still popular."

Kathleen Norris

"Success to me is having ten honeydew melons and eating only the top half of each one."

Barbara Streisand

"I keep the telephone of my mind open to peace, harmony, health, love and abundance. Then whenever doubt, anxiety, or fear try to call me, they keep getting a busy signal and soon they'll forget my number."

Edith Armstrong

"I don't know anything about luck. I've never banked on it, and I'm afraid of people who do. Luck to me is something else; hard work and realizing what is opportunity and what isn't."

Lucille Ball

"Ninety-eight percent of the adults in this country are decent, hard-working, honest Americans. It's the other lousy two percent that get all the publicity.
But then we elected them."

Lily Tomlin

"Sometimes when I look at my children I say to myself, 'Lillian, you should have stayed a virgin.'"

Lillian Carter

"I never hated a man enough to give him his diamonds back."

Zsa Zsa Gabor

"I've been rich &
I've been poor.
Rich is better."

Sophie Tucker

"Remember,
no one can make
you feel inferior
without your
consent."

Eleanor Roosevelt

"To be successful, a woman has to be better at her job than a man."

Golda Meir

"I'm just a person trapped inside a woman's body."

Elaine Boosler

"An archeologist is the best
husband a woman can
have; the older she gets,
the more interested
he is in her."

Agatha Christie

"Some people are more turned on by money than they are by love...In one respect they're alike. They're both wonderful as long as they last."

Abigail VanBuren

"In society it is etiquette for ladies to have the best chairs and get handed things.
In the home the reverse is the case. That is why ladies are more sociable than gentlemen."

Virginia Graham

"You don't seem to realize that a poor person who is unhappy is in a better position than a rich person who is unhappy. Because the poor person has hope. He thinks money would help."

Jean Kerr

"Laziness may appear attractive, but work gives satisfaction."

Anne Frank

"The important thing in acting
is to be able to laugh and cry.
If I have to cry,
I think of my sex life.
If I have to laugh,
I think of my sex life."

Glenda Jackson

"Old age is like a plane
flying through a storm.
Once you're aboard,
there's nothing
you can do."

Golda Meir

"The suburbs were discovered, quite by accident, one day in the early 1940s by a Welcome Wagon lady who was lost."

Erma Bombeck

"The trouble with the
rat race is that
even if you win,
you're still a rat."

Lily Tomlin

"It's easy to be
independent when
you've got money.
But to be independent
when you haven't got
a thing—
that's the Lord's test."

Mahalia Jackson

"I don't want to
  live—I want to love
  first, and live
  incidentally."

Zelda Fitzgerald

Other Great Quotations Books:

- Best of Success
- Business Quotes
- Commitment to Excellence
- Commitment to Quality
- Customer Care
- Golf Quotes
- Great Quotes/Great Leaders
- Great Quotes/Great Women
- Management Magic
- Motivational Quotes
- Opportunity Selling
- Think
- What Motivates People
- Winning Words

GREAT QUOTATIONS, INC.
919 SPRINGER DRIVE • LOMBARD, IL 60148-6416

TOLL FREE: 800-621-1432 (outside Illinois)
(312) 953-1222

PRINTED IN U.S.A.